I0693904

"Thou art a boil, a plague sore, an embossed carbuncle"

IN *KING LEAR*, WILLIAM SHAKESPEARE

HOW TO NEVER SAY F*CK AGAIN

A LITTLE GUIDE TO POLITE AND CREATIVE INSULTS

FUN AND GAMES TO BECOME A MASTER INSULT DUELLIST WITH CLASS

IF YOU THOUGHT THAT WAS ABOUT BEING POLITE, YOU WERE WRONG. PARTLY. BECAUSE IT'S ALL ABOUT CHOOSING THE RIGHT WORDS AND BEING CREATIVE. GIVE A VIBE. PAINT AN IMAGE.

LET'S TRY.

LET'S START THE EASY WAY.

TELL ME NOW. WHAT ARE YOUR FAVOURITE INSULTS?
AND PLEASE INCLUDE FUCK, BECAUSE IT'S AN AMAZING WORD.
I PROMISE I WON'T TELL ANYBODY.

Best Victorian Insults

1. "YOU, SIR, ARE AN EGREGIOUS ASS!"
2. "TURN DOWN THE VOLUME, CHURCH BELL!" (TALKATIVE WOMAN)
3. "YOU ARE A NINCOMPOOP!"
4. "YOU ARE A BUFFOON, A DOLT, AND A SCOUNDREL!"
5. "YOU HAVE THE MORALS OF AN ALLEY CAT AND THE MANNERS OF A PIG!"
6. "YOU ARE A SCURRILOUS KNAVE AND A CONSUMMATE CHEAT!"
7. "MAY THE FLEAS OF A THOUSAND CAMELS INFEST YOUR ARMPITS!"
8. "YOU ARE A WANTON CRETIN!"
9. "YOU ARE A TERMAGANT, AND A FOOL!" (SHREW)
10. "YOU ARE A CONTEMPTIBLE CUR AND A SCROFULOUS WRETCH!"
11. "YOU PERFIDIOUS VALET!"
12. "YOU ARE A DECEITFUL ROGUE!"
13. "MAY THE RATS OF THE SEWERS FEAST ON YOUR ENTRAILS!"
14. "YOU ARE A SIMPERING FOOL AND A BLATHERING IDIOT!"
15. "MAY YOU BE STRUCK BY LIGHTNING AND DEVOURED BY WOLVES!"
16. "YOU ARE A SPINELESS JELLYFISH!"
17. "YOU PUSILLANIMOUS COWARD!"
18. "YOU ARE A SLANDEROUS CURMUDGEON AND A MALICIOUS MISCREANT!"
19. "YOU INCOMPETENT FOOZLER!"
20. "YOU ARE A VILE WRETCH AND A LOATHSOME INSECT!"

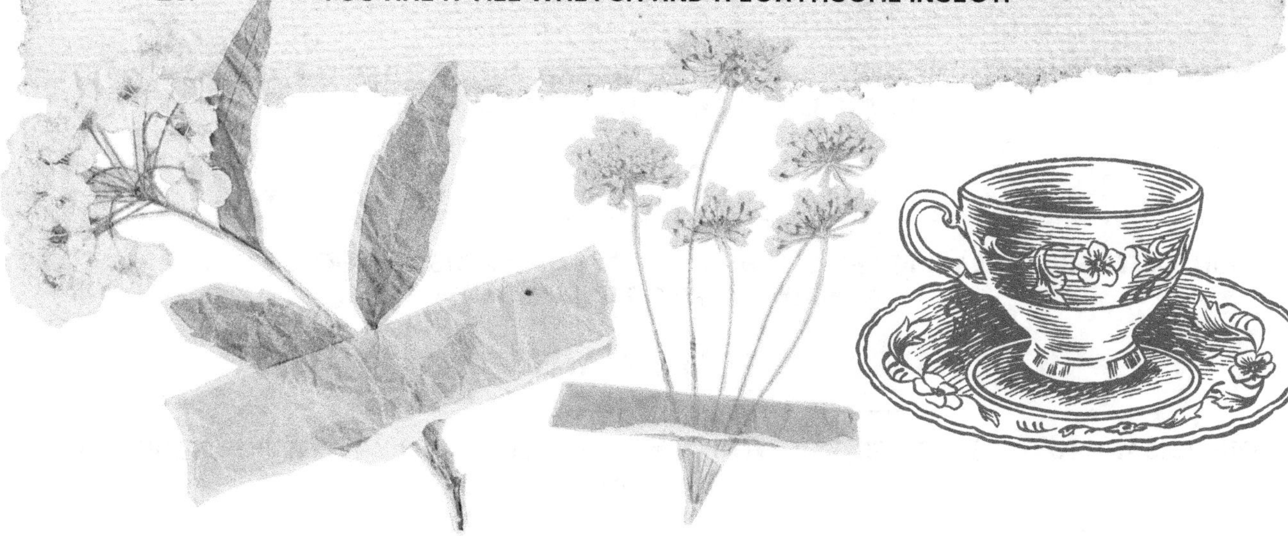

OH WAIT ! ONE VERY IMPORTANT THING BEFORE WE GO FURTHER.
NEVER USE A WORD YOU DON'T UNDERSTAND !

SO LET'S TAKE A LOOK AT SOME OF THOSE WORDS

EGREGIOUS

ADJECTIVE (FORMAL DISAPPROVING) - MEANING : EXTREMELY BAD IN A WAY THAT IS VERY NOTICEABLE

NINCOMPOOP

NOUN (INFORMAL) - MEANING : A SILLY OR STUPID PERSON

DOLT

NOUN (DISAPPROVING) - MEANING : A STUPID PERSON

SCURRILOUS

ADJECTIVE (FORMAL) - MEANING : EXPRESSING UNFAIR OR FALSE CRITICISM THAT IS LIKELY TO DAMAGE SOMEONE'S REPUTATION

KNAVE

NOUN (OLD USE) - MEANING : A DISHONEST MAN

CONSUMMATE

ADJECTIVE [BEFORE NOUN] (FORMAL) - MEANING : PERFECT, OR COMPLETE IN EVERY WAY

WANTON

ADJECTIVE (FORMAL) - MEANING : (OF SOMETHING BAD, SUCH AS DAMAGE, CRUELTY, WASTE) EXTREME AND SHOWING NO CARE AT ALL

CRETIN

NOUN (OFFENSIVE) - MEANING : AN OFFENSIVE WORD FOR A PERSON WHO IS CONSIDERED TO BE VERY STUPID OR UNPLEASANT

TERMAGANT

NOUN (DISAPPROVING) - MEANING : A WOMAN WHO ARGUES NOISILY TO GET OR ACHIEVE WHAT SHE WANTS

CUR

NOUN (LITERARY) - MEANING : A MONGREL (= DOG OF MIXED TYPE), ESPECIALLY ONE THAT IS FRIGHTENING OR FIERCE

SCROFULOUS

ADJECTIVE - MEANING : MORALLY CONTAMINATED

ROGUE

NOUN (OLD-FASHIONED HUMOROUS) - MEANING : A PERSON WHO BEHAVES BADLY BUT WHO YOU STILL LIKE

SIMPER

VERB [I] - MEANING : TO SMILE IN A SILLY OR ANNOYING WAY

BLATHER

VERB [I] - MEANING : TO TALK FOR A LONG TIME IN A SILLY OR ANNOYING WAY

PUSILLANIMOUS

ADJECTIVE (FORMAL) - MEANING : WEAK AND COWARDLY (= NOT BRAVE); FRIGHTENED OF TAKING RISKS

SLANDEROUS

ADJECTIVE - MEANING : FALSE, AND DAMAGING TO SOMEONE'S REPUTATION

CURMUDGEON

NOUN (OLD-FASHIONED) - MEANING : AN OLD PERSON WHO IS OFTEN IN A BAD MOOD

FOOZLER (OLD) OR BUNGLER

NOUN - MEANING : A PERSON WHO DOES SOMETHING VERY BADLY, IN A CARELESS OR STUPID WAY

WHAT ARE THE BEST 10 INSULTS YOUR FRIENDS ARE USING? ASK AND HAVE FUN.

#@©!⚡
*⫽©!◁
F@!!#

ALTERNATIVES TO STUPID :

NINCOMPOOP
AIRHEAD
BERK
DUNDERHEAD
DUNCE
TOSSER
DOLT
DULLARD
BIRDBRAIN
BUNGLER
DIMWIT
LUG
LUMMOX
HOSER
KLUTZ
SCHMUCK
NITWIT
PIPSQUEAK
TWIRP
SIMP
PUTZ
OAF
BUFFOON
CHUMP
CRACKPOT
CRANK
CRETIN
DOOFUS
DIVVY
EEJIT

FLIBBERTIGIBBET
IGNORAMUS
NINNY
PILLOCK
VAZEY

LIST YOUR 10 FAVES

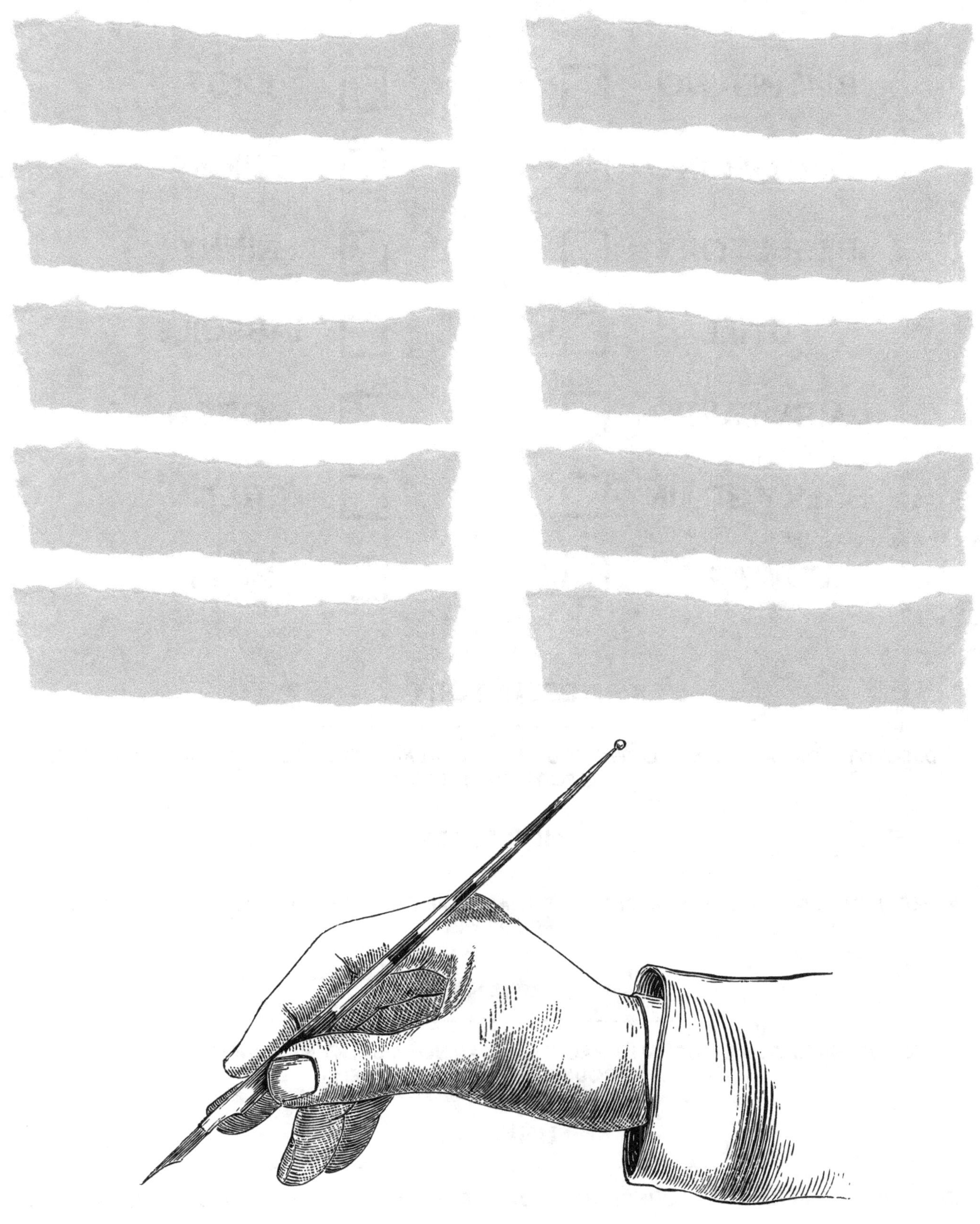

MIX & MATCH GAME

HAVE FUN WITH VERBS AND ADJECTIVES ! WHAT CAN YOU ADD TO IDIOT
TO MAKE IT YOURS? ASSOCIATE WORDS TO YOUR LIKING.

BLITHERING	☐	☐	IDIOT
SNIGGERING	☐	☐	DUMMY
DESULTORY	☐	☐	NINNY
FUTILE	☐	☐	IMBECILE
AIRY-FAIRY	☐	☐	MORON
BALKY BRAIN	☐	☐	CRETIN
UNWARY	☐	☐	MUTT

DESULTORY

ADJECTIVE (FORMAL) - MEANING : WITHOUT A CLEAR PLAN OR PURPOSE AND SHOWING LITTLE
EFFORT OR INTEREST

AIRY-FAIRY

ADJECTIVE (UK INFORMAL) - MEANING : NOT PRACTICAL OR NOT BASED ON THE SITUATION AS IT
REALLY IS

BALKY

ADJECTIVE (MAINLY US. UK USUALLY BAULKY) - MEANING : A BALKY MACHINE, DEVICE, OR PART OF
THE BODY IS NOT WORKING WELL

UNWARY

ADJECTIVE - MEANING : NOT CONSCIOUS OF OR CAREFUL ABOUT POSSIBLE RISKS AND DANGERS

ALTERNATIVES TO COWARD

PANTYWAIST, N.
CHICKEN, N.
LILY-LIVERED, ADJ.
TIMOROUS, ADJ.
YELLOW-BELLIED, ADJ.
CRAVEN, ADJ.

FOR MEAN FELLOWS

CAD

NOUN (OLD-FASHIONED) - MEANING : A MAN WHO BEHAVES BADLY OR DISHONESTLY, ESPECIALLY TO WOMEN

BLACKGUARD

NOUN (OLD-FASHIONED) - MEANING : A PERSON, USUALLY A MAN, WHO IS NOT HONEST OR FAIR AND HAS NO MORAL PRINCIPLES

SKINFLINT

NOUN (INFORMAL DISAPPROVING) - MEANING : A PERSON WHO IS UNWILLING TO SPEND MONEY

ABYSMAL

ADJECTIVE (BAD) - MEANING : VERY BAD

CHURLISH

ADJECTIVE - MEANING : RUDE, UNFRIENDLY, AND UNPLEASANT

WHAT ABOUT ANIMALS?

GALLINIPPER

NOUN (CHIEFLY SOUTHERN US AND MIDLAND US) - MEANING : ANY OF VARIOUS INSECTS (SUCH AS A LARGE MOSQUITO OR CRANE FLY) / ONE WHO SMELLS OF FARTS

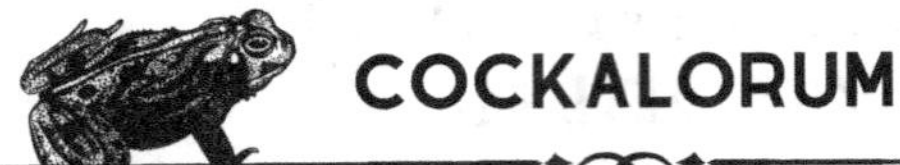

COCKALORUM

NOUN - MEANING : A BOASTFUL AND SELF-IMPORTANT PERSON / LEAPFROG

VULTURE

PEACOCK

WOODCOCK

NOUN - MEANING : ONE OF TWO DISTINCT BIRDS OF THE FAMILY SCOLOPACIDÆ, CLOSELY RELATED TO THE TRUE SNIPE (GALLINAGO) / NOUN OBSOLETE FIG.: A SIMPLETON.

POPINJAY

JACKAL

GRIMALKIN

NOUN - MEANING : OLD CAT, ESPECIALLY A SHE-CAT / A BAD-TEMPERED OLD WOMAN.

GADFLY

NOUN - MEANING : A PERSISTENT IRRITATING CRITIC; A NUISANCE / ONE THAT ACTS AS A PROVOCATIVE STIMULUS / A GOAD.

BUZZARD

NOUN - MEANING : ANY OF VARIOUS NORTH AMERICAN VULTURES, SUCH AS THE TURKEY VULTURE / NOUN AN AVARICIOUS OR OTHERWISE UNPLEASANT PERSON.

THE ONES I USE NOT IN THE LIST :

ALTERNATIVE TO SHIT / FUCK

26 IS MY PERSONAL FAVE

1. WHOOPSIDAISIES
2. DARN IT
3. GOODNESS
4. OH DEAR
5. CRAP
6. GOSH DARN IT
7. FIDDLESTICKS
8. HOLY COW
9. HECK
10. DRAT
11. GOOD GRIEF
12. OH BOTHER
13. SUGAR
14. DAG NABBIT
15. OH FUDGE
16. MERCY ME
17. GREAT SCOTT
18. GOOD GOLLY
19. BY GUM
20. GEE WHIZ
21. HOLY MOLY
22. BLIMEY
23. CRIKEY
24. FANCY THAT
25. STONE THE CROWS
26. BUTTER MY BUTT AND CALL ME A BISCUIT
27. YOU DON'T SAY
28. JUMPING JEHOSHAPHAT
29. DRAT
30. BLAST
31. DAGNABBIT
32. SHOOT
33. SHUCKS
34. TARNATION
35. CRIPES
36. DANG
37. PISH
38. RATS
39. BLOOMING HECK
40. FOR MERCY'S SAKE

LIST YOUR 10 FAVES

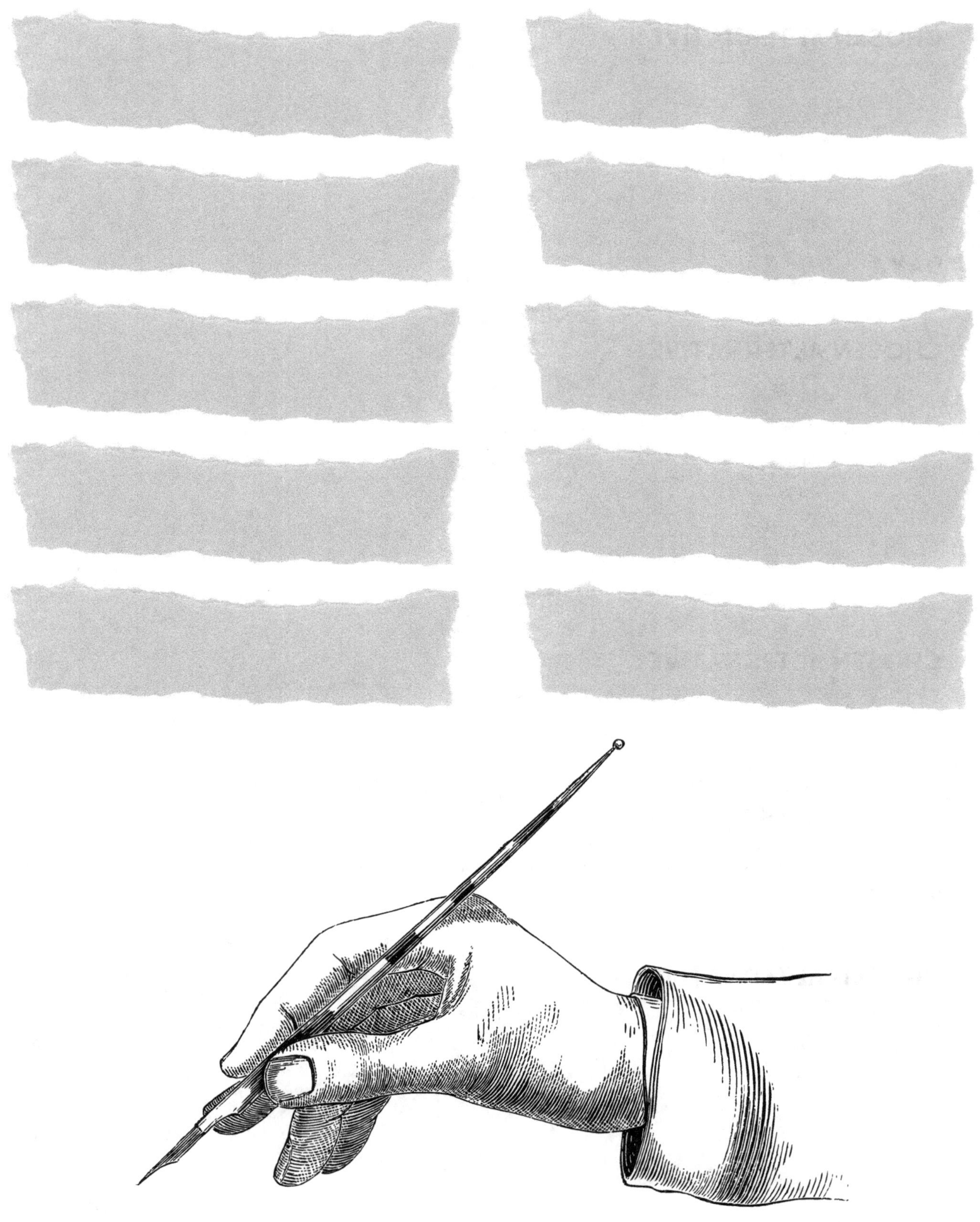

THE WEEKLY CHALLENGE
PICK ONE ALTERNATIVE TO FUCK AND TRY IT FOR A DAY

CHOSEN ALTERNATIVE :

DAY 1

CHOSEN ALTERNATIVE :

DAY 2

CHOSEN ALTERNATIVE :

DAY 3

CHOSEN ALTERNATIVE :

DAY 4

THE WEEKLY CHALLENGE
PICK ONE ALTERNATIVE TO FUCK AND TRY IT FOR A DAY

CHOSEN ALTERNATIVE :

DAY 5

CHOSEN ALTERNATIVE :

DAY 6

CHOSEN ALTERNATIVE :

DAY 7

MY CONCLUSION :

DON'T BE AFRAID OF PLEONASMS. THEY ARE BLOODY FUNNY.

PLEONASM

NOUN - MEANING : THE USE OF MORE WORDS THAN ARE NEEDED TO EXPRESS A MEANING, DONE EITHER UNINTENTIONALLY OR FOR EMPHASIS.

MIX AND MATCH TO YOUR LIKING

EMPTY-HEADED	☐	☐	LUMMOX
DOPEY	☐	☐	HOSER
ABSURD	☐	☐	KLUTZ
BATTY	☐	☐	SCHMUCK
DIPPY	☐	☐	NITWIT
DAFFY	☐	☐	PIPSQUEAK
GULLIBLE	☐	☐	TWIRP
IDIOTIC	☐	☐	SIMP
LUMPISH	☐	☐	PUTZ
MINDLESS	☐	☐	DOOFUS
MORONIC	☐	☐	DIVVY
FARCICAL	☐	☐	EEJIT
OBTUSE	☐	☐	FLIBBERTIGIBBET
ILLOGICAL	☐	☐	IGNORAMUS
VAPID	☐	☐	NINNY

LET'S MAKE YOUR OWN LIST

WHAT CAN YOU FIND IN THE DICTIONARY THAT COULD BE TURNED INTO AN INSULT? MY FAVE WOULD BE "DEGENERATED BIPEDE". WORKS QUITE WELL TO EXPRESS DESPISE.

PARDON MY FRENCH !

OK, LET'S SEE WHAT THE FRENCH HAS TO SAY. THEY'RE SUPPOSED TO BE EXPERTS, AREN'T THEY?

1. CONNARD
2. VA TE FAIRE FOUTRE
3. FERME TA GUEULE
4. FAIS CHIER
5. BÂTARD
6. TROU DU CUL
7. SAC À MERDE
8. CASSE-COUILLES
9. ENFOIRÉ
10. PÉTASSE
11. ABRUTI
12. COUILLON
13. CRÉTIN
14. DÉBILE
15. PAUVRE CON
16. TOCARD
17. SALE MERDE
18. POUFFIASSE
19. VA TE FAIRE CUIRE LE CUL
20. BOUFFON

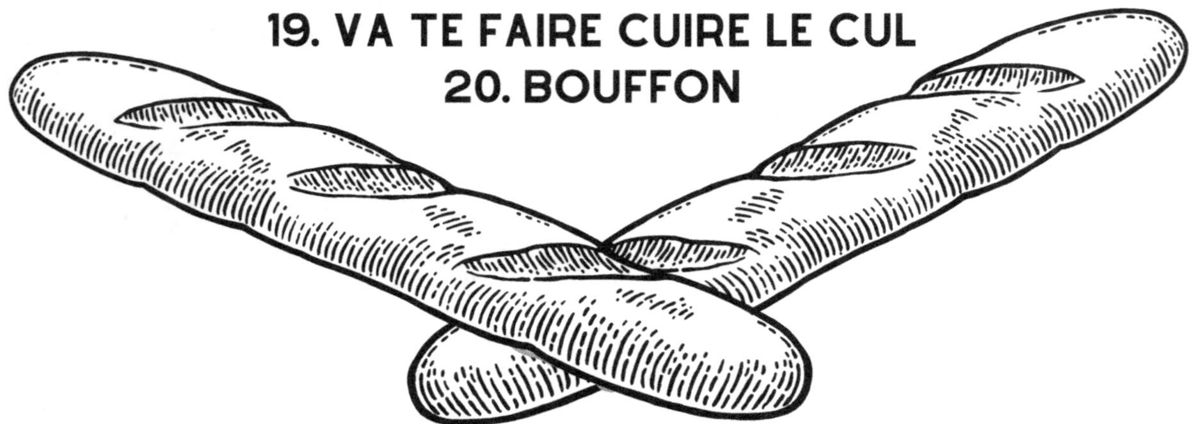

PARDON MY FRENCH !

OK, LET'S SEE WHAT THE FRENCH HAS TO SAY. THEY'RE SUPPOSED TO BE EXPERTS, AREN'T THEY?

FUN AND GAMES : TRY TO PRONOUNCE THIS WHOLE LIST OF FRENCH INSULTS !

MEANING

1. JERK
2. FUCK OFF
3. SHUT UP
4. CRAP
5. BASTARD
6. ASSHOLE
7. SHITBAG
8. PAIN IN THE ASS
(LITERALLY : SOMEONE TEDIOUS ENOUGH TO "BREAK" SOMEONE'S BALLS)
9. ARSEHOLE/BASTARD
10. BITCH
11. MORON
12. HALFWIT/SCHMUCK
13. NUMBSKULL
14. MUPPET/NUMPTY/MORON
15. DUMBASS
16. LOSER
17. MISERABLE SHIT
18. FLOOZY
19. GET LOST
(BUT IT ACTUALLY IMPLIES THAT YOU MANAGE TO PUT YOUR ASS IN A VERY HOT PAN DOING THAT)
20. BUFFOON

Merci

TIME TRAVEL
WHAT ABOUT MEDIEVAL FRENCH INSULTS? THEY'RE A BIT HARDER. EXPERT LEVEL ONLY

1. BÉLÎTRE
2. BUTOR
3. CUISTRE
4. FAQUIN
5. ORCHIDOCLASTE
6. FARAUD
7. NODOCÉPHALE
8. FORBAN
9. FRIPON
10. GODICHE
11. GOUGNAFIER
12. JEAN-FOUTRE
13. MARAUD
14. MALOTRU
15. MUFLE
16. PALTOQUET
17. PIGNOUF
18. POURCEAU
19. RIBAUD
20. SAGOUIN

TIME TRAVEL
WHAT ABOUT MEDIEVAL FRENCH
INSULTS? THEY'RE A BIT HARDER.
EXPERT LEVEL ONLY

1. IGNORANT MAN
2. OAF
3. PRIG
4. KNAVE
5. PAIN IN THE ASS / JERK
SAME AS CASSE-COUILLES BUT WITH ANCIENT GREEK WORDS. CLASSY.
6. BRAGGART / BLUSTERER
7. VERY POLITE WAY TO SAY DICKHEAD
WITH BOTH LATIN AND ANCIENT GREEK WORDS.
8. BANDIT / CROOK
9. RASCAL / ROGUE
10. AWKWARD
11. WORTHLESS MAN
12. LAYABOUT / WASTREL / USELESS IDIOT
13. RASCAL / SCOUNDREL
14. PHILISTINE / OAF
15. BOOR / LOUT
16. CHEEKY DISRESPECTFUL MAN
17. YOKEL / CLODHOPPER / DIMWIT
18. PIG.
19. PROSTITUTE
20. SLOB

CAN YOUR FRIENDS GUESS WHAT THOSE WORDS MEAN?

YOU WANT TO MAKE IT RANDOM?

NO PROBLEM. CUT THOSE PAPERS AND PUT THEM IN A BOX/ BAG/PENCIL CASE. AND SORT ONE RANDOM WHEN YOU NEED TO EXPRESS IMPOLITE THOUGHTS!

WHOOPSIDAISIES	FIDDLESTICKS	DAG NABBIT
OH FUDGE	GREAT SCOTT	MERCY ME
GEE WHIZ	BLIMEY	STONE THE CROWS!
BUTTER MY BUTT AND CALL ME A BISCUIT	JUMPING JEHOSHAPHAT	DAGNABBIT
TARNATION	BLOOMING HECK	PISH

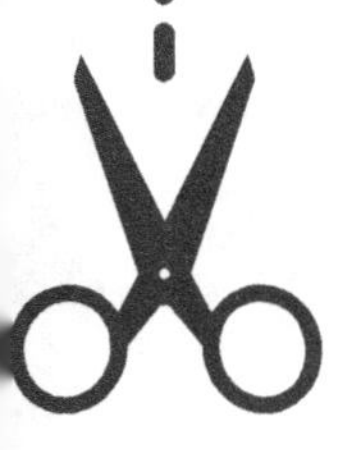

YOU WANT TO MAKE IT RANDOM?

NO PROBLEM. CUT THOSE PAPERS AND PUT THEM IN A BOX/ BAG/PENCIL CASE. AND SORT ONE RANDOM WHEN YOU NEED TO EXPRESS IMPOLITE THOUGHTS!

NINCOMPOOP	LUMMOX	DIVVY
AIRHEAD	FLIBBERTIGIBBET	IGNORAMUS
VAZEY	BIRDBRAIN	NITWIT
EEJIT	SIMP	PIPSQUEAK
DOOFUS	SCHMUCK	LUG

YOU WANT TO MAKE IT PERSONAL?

NO PROBLEM. CUT THOSE PAPERS AND PUT THEM IN A BOX/ BAG/PENCIL CASE. AND SORT ONE RANDOM WHEN YOU NEED TO EXPRESS IMPOLITE THOUGHTS!

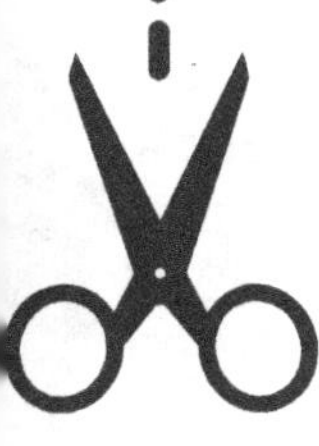

YOU WANT TO MAKE IT PERSONAL?

NO PROBLEM. CUT THOSE PAPERS AND PUT THEM IN A BOX/ BAG/PENCIL CASE. AND SORT ONE RANDOM WHEN YOU NEED TO EXPRESS IMPOLITE THOUGHTS!

YOU WANT TO MAKE IT PERSONAL?

NO PROBLEM. CUT THOSE PAPERS AND PUT THEM IN A BOX/ BAG/PENCIL CASE. AND SORT ONE RANDOM WHEN YOU NEED TO EXPRESS IMPOLITE THOUGHTS!

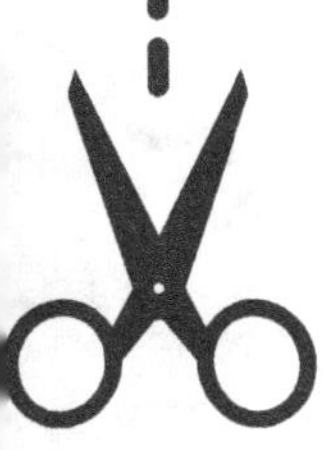

THERE YOU ARE !

I HOPE YOU HAD FUN WITH THIS LITTLE BOOK ! AND DON'T FORGET THAT
IT'S ALWAYS GOOD TO HAVE A NICE WORD HERE AND THERE!

SOURCES : CAMBRIDGE DICTIONARY & MERRIAM-WEBSTER DICTIONARY